Using stories
to teach
Science

Ages 5–6

A division of MA Education Ltd

Steve Way visits schools presenting his science stories, maths stories and creative writing ideas. He gained a degree in Biological Sciences at Lancaster University before studying for his P.G.C.E.

Simon Hickton is Headteacher of Carcroft Primary School near Doncaster. He gained a degree in Biochemistry from York University before studying for his P.G.C.E..

Published by Hopscotch, A division of MA Education Ltd
St Jude's Church, Dulwich Road,
Herne Hill, London SE24 0PB
Tel: 020 7738 5454

© 2008 MA Education Ltd

Written by Steve Way and Simon Hickton
Series design by Blade Communications
Cover illustration by Debbie Clark
Illustrated by John Welding
Printed in the UK by CLE

ISBN 978-1-90539-024-3

Steve Way and Simon Hickton hereby assert their moral right to be identified as the authors of this work in accordance with the Copyright, Designs and Patents Act, 1988.

Contents

Introduction   4

Ourselves   5

Growing plants   13

Materials   21

Light and dark   28

Pushes and pulls   36

Sound and hearing   44

Problems for Princess Puzzle   52

Notes on the story 'Problems for Princess   56
Puzzle' (a story on the theme of fair testing)

Introduction

About the series

The two books in the Key Stage 1 series *Using stories to teach science* use stories as a different but fun way of initiating a science lesson. The aim is for a science concept to be presented in a format that shows how science can relate to normal (or imagined!) life. The more ways, especially fun ways, we look at a subject we are learning, the more likely we are to come to understand it and to remember it!

Each book includes one story for each of the six main units of study in the DfES *Scheme of Work for Science* that the children have to cover in science in that year, along with a suggested lesson plan and photocopiable resource sheets. These sheets are sometimes activity sheets or in other cases recording sheets. In each case, the story and its associated lesson could be used to introduce each unit or could be incorporated into the series of lessons you are planning for that unit of study. The suggested lesson plans are only a guide and so you can pick and choose the suggestions and ideas that will work best in your school or with your class.

Reading the story

When you read the story to the children, we recommend that you read it twice; the first time as a story in its truest sense – one they can listen to and enjoy as a piece of narrative, without it being broken up and dissected as it's told. Hopefully, the enjoyment they get from the story will enhance their enjoyment of the science they will be learning. However, on the first reading of the story, they may have been so involved in the plot and characters that they miss some of the science ideas that are used. So on the second reading you can get the children to focus on the science ideas that are woven into the story, by stopping at the points where a new science concept enters into the narrative and discussing its role in the story. If at all possible, enlarge a copy of the story and display it on an overhead projector as you are reading it. The children will then have the benefit of seeing the illustrations as you read and some may even be able to follow the text with you.

One extra story

'Problems for Princess Puzzle', on page 52, is an additional story on the theme of fair testing. It has been provided for you to use in a science lesson of your own devising (see the notes on page 56).

Using the lesson plans

Each lesson plan contains:
- ❑ The learning objectives, with the National Curriculum and Scheme of Work references;
- ❑ A list of the resources required;
- ❑ Whole class starter activities;
- ❑ Suggestions for individual, paired or group work;
- ❑ A plenary session;
- ❑ Further suggestions.

There are also three characters, known as WALT, WILF and TIB, who provide information.

 WALT stands for 'We Are Learning Today'.

 WILF stands for 'What I'm Looking For'.

 TIB stands for 'This Is Because'.

These or similar systems are often used to ensure lessons are focused, objective led and in context for the learner. They help summarise the purpose of the lesson, what is required of the children in order for them to successfully learn that lesson and why what they are learning is important.

The resource sheets have been designed to support the learning the children are making in science. Completing them will often require literacy skills, which in some cases the children will not have acquired as yet. In order that the work remains focused on science, we suggest that you, or your classroom assistants, scribe for such children so that their capability in science is not held back by specific difficulties with literacy. The investigative lessons support assessment for learning by enabling time for teachers and/or classroom assistants to record comments made by the children as they plan experiments, discuss predictions and so on.

We hope you enjoy using this book and that the ideas in it help add to your toolbox of resources for teaching science.

Science Scheme of Work objective

Unit 1A: Ourselves

Section 2: The five senses

To be taught 'about the senses that enable humans and other animals to be aware of the world around them'.

NC Sc2 2g

Background

This chapter allows the children to explore for themselves and think about the five senses that we possess and also the senses possessed by some animals, along with providing opportunities for class discussion of the five senses.

The story and the follow-up work the children do will provide them with tools, such as images they can recall, to learn and remember the five senses of touch, smell, taste, hearing and sight. They provide a stimulus to encourage the children to appreciate their senses and think about how we benefit from having them. It also reminds us to think about the importance of maintaining good health, so that we can maintain our senses and to think about people who have one or two senses that are less acute or missing and how to appreciate and help them.

Resources

• Photocopiable activity sheets 1–3 (pages 10–12)

What to do

We are learning about the five senses.

❏ Explain to the children that the lesson will involve them thinking about the five senses that we and some animals possess that enable us to be aware of the world around us. To demonstrate the senses you could get the children to use each one and then list them. For example:

• For **touch** – ask one or more of the children to close their eyes and then give them a furry toy to hold. Ask them to describe it; then ask them how they were able to describe it.

• For **taste** – as above but this time give each child a piece of biscuit to eat. Ask them to tell you how they knew it was a biscuit.

• For **hearing** – give the children instructions such as 'Stand up' and 'Sit down.' Ask them how they knew what you wanted them to do.

• For **sight** – say, 'Look at that,' and point to something interesting in the classroom, possibly something unusual you've placed in an unexpected location (such as on the ceiling!) that they wouldn't have noticed otherwise. Ask the children how they managed to notice the object.

• For **smell** – ask the children to close their eyes. Spray a small amount of perfume into the air. Ask them to tell you what you did and how they were able to tell.

❏ Tell the children that the story is about a funny professor who seems to have forgotten that people have different senses that help them know about what's going on in the world around us. He's trying to make a machine that will help us know about the world around us, using senses we already have! Tell them to listen to the story carefully because they will be making drawings of the machine the professor is trying to make or machines similar to it.

❏ Read the story (pages 7–9).

❏ Ask the children if they can remember which senses the professor's machine was supposed to have and which animal he was using as the inspiration for each part of his machine. List them as you go, asking the children why the professor used each animal as the inspiration for that part. Ask them why that particular sense is so useful to that animal and also why that sense is so useful to us.

❏ You could also ask the children to think about all the ways the senses help us today to find out about what's going on in the environment around us – which often involves avoiding danger. For example, seeing and hearing that a car is coming! You could make a class list of the ways in which each sense is useful.

Ourselves

We're going to draw a robot like the one in the story, showing each of the five senses.

We need to understand how incredible we are.

Further suggestions

- The children could be asked to draw a mind map of the five senses particularly thinking about what we use our senses for; for example, ears to hear the alarm clock in the morning so we can get to school on time (hooray!).

Individual, paired or group work

❏ Explain to the children that you now want them to make their own drawing of the Robo-Octopus-Dog-Rat-Bat-Eagle-ot or a robot inspired by other animals likely to have, or well known for having, each of the five senses. Hand out Activity sheet 1, 2 or 3. Ask them to label their drawing, showing which part of their drawing represents each sense.

❏ Activity sheet 1 is for lower attainers. It requires the children to draw a Robo-Octopus-Dog-Rat-Bat-Eagle-ot and gives illustrated and verbal reminders of the five senses they have to include and label. The average attainer sheet (sheet 2) only gives illustrated reminders while the higher attainer sheet (sheet 3) asks the children to make up their own robot, using different animals as their inspiration without any reminders about the senses that need to be labelled.

❏ You could cut out the pictures they have drawn and use them for a classroom display.

Plenary

❏ Ask the children to list the five senses. Discuss the ways in which each sense is particularly useful to us and why we should appreciate having it; for example, how it can make life more rewarding and protect us from danger. Refer back to the class list if you made one. You could ask the children to think about how we should help and appreciate those people who have sensory impairments of some kind and think about how we can help them to be safe and to enjoy the senses that they have. You could also discuss how important it is to protect our sense organs such as the eyes and ears and how they can be protected when we do certain jobs.

'WHIZZ!!! Ka-ching! Zipp! BONG!'

'OH BOTHER, BOTHER BOTHER!!!'

'What's he up to this time?' thought Stir-Fry as he was taking the professor's dinner to him in his laboratory.

When he opened the door he was none the wiser. The professor was dwarfed by his attempt at a latest invention. All Stir-Fry could see were mechanical models of tentacles, noses, tongues, wings, legs, eyes, ears and so on, all sticking out in all directions. It looked like a nightmare made up of a mad mix of lots of animals.

'Ah, Stir-Fry,' said Professor Darius Mc Von Wibble Wibble. 'This is my latest invention… well, latest invention to be… it's a "Robo-Octopus-Dog-Rat-Bat-Eagle-ot"!'

'Um.. what does it do… or rather what is it supposed to do?' asked Stir-Fry, pretty sure that the answer was going to be fairly nutty.

'I'm making a device that can see, hear, feel, taste and smell!' The professor explained. 'The octopus is famous for its sense of touch – after all, it's got eight tentacles to feel with! Dogs are often used to help us because of their strong sense of smell.

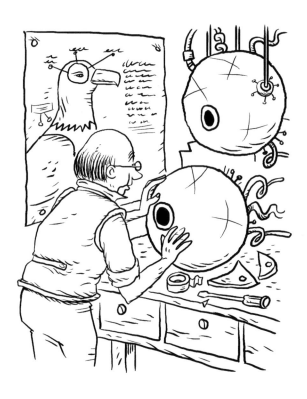

Rats have a brilliant sense of taste so they can tell if something is good to eat or not, bats have a terrific sense of hearing as it helps them fly in the dark and eagles are… well… eagle-eyed, ha ha, because their sharp sense of sight helps them find their food!

My machine will have all these five incredible senses! It'll know all sorts of amazing things about what's going on around it! I'll just have to feed it healthy fuel – known as food – and give it plenty of chance to keep all its parts working – known as "exercise"!'

'Um…' began Stir-Fry, nervously. He knew the professor hated anyone not liking his inventions – no matter how crazy they were. 'Aren't you just trying to invent a machine that does what most people can do anyway?' he asked.

'What do you mean?' demanded the professor.

'Well, most people already have all of those five incredible senses of sight, hearing, touch, smell and taste. Also, most people lacking one or two senses can use the ones they have even more strongly anyway. For people to keep healthy they have to eat healthy food and have exercise, just like your robo-thingy-ot,' explained Stir-Fry.

When Stir-Fry had finished there was silence for a while. The only sound was made by a bit of the professor's invention as it fell off and hit the ground.

'Hmm,' said the professor eventually. 'It does seem that people can do all the things that my "Robo-Octopus-Dog-Rat-Bat-Eagle-ot" can do.'

'Er. Yes…' agreed Stir-Fry as another part of the invention fell off. 'I'm sure it'll come in useful for something though!' he added.

'Yes… yes…' agreed the professor. 'Maybe I'll have a go at inventing something else. No use inventing something people can do by themselves already.'

'Good idea,' agreed Stir-Fry.

A few days later, the professor was starting to invent a machine that helps you put your socks on. Meanwhile, Stir-Fry was hanging the washing out to dry on the bits sticking out of the "Robo-Octopus-Dog-Rat-Bat-Eagle-ot" that hadn't ended up falling off it.

Name _____

My Robo-Octopus-Dog-Rat-Bat-Eagle-ot

Draw a picture of what you think the
Robo-Octopus-Dog-Rat-Bat-Eagle-ot
would look like.

Label each of the senses that the machine would have.
There are clues at the bottom of the page to help you.

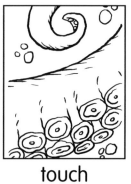				
touch	smell	taste	hearing	sight

Name _____

My senses machine

Draw a picture of the robot with five senses from the story or your own machine.

Label each of the senses that the machine would have.

There are clues at the bottom of the page to help you.

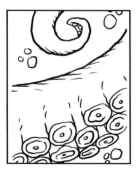
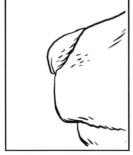

Name _____

My senses machine

Draw a picture of a different machine with five senses,
using different animals as the idea behind each part.
Label each of the senses that the machine would have.

The name of my machine is _____

Growing plants

Science Scheme of Work objectives

Unit 1B: Growing plants.

Section 5: Watering plants

Section 6: Plants and light

To conclude that plants need water to grow.

To present results by writing or drawing in a table or chart prepared for them.

NC Sc2 3a, 3b, 3c

Background

This chapter explores the needs of plants in a humorous way, comparing their needs with our own, which neatly refers back to Unit 1A: Ourselves, which all Year 1 units are supposed to do. The follow-up work outlines an experiment looking at the effect of water on the growth of seeds.

One interesting aspect of this activity is that many children think plants need soil in order to grow but they will notice that the seeds germinate on cotton wool. The differentiated activity sheets could also be used for the recording of results of experiments looking at the effect of light on growth or other experiments suggested and designed by the children. The recording of results is an important part of this unit.

Plants need water to germinate as, when it is taken up by the seeds, it rehydrates the cells that were largely dehydrated as the seeds were formed. This allows enzymes in the cells to become active, particularly the ones that allow the food stores to be used for new growth. Perhaps surprisingly, seeds also need oxygen though, so if the seeds are waterlogged, as in one set of experiments suggested here, they won't be able to get any oxygen and are unlikely to grow.

Resources

- Photocopiable record sheets 1–3 (pages 18–20)
- Seeds such as cress, sunflower, marrow (note: seeds from garden centres may have been treated with pesticides; seeds from health food shops are normally safe)
- Cotton wool
- Teaspoons (8)
- Labels (8)
- Containers to grow seeds in – for example, either petri dishes or chip-shop trays
- Measured quantities of water x2 (enough to quarter fill the container, half fill the container and completely fill the container)

What to do

We are learning about what seeds need to grow.

- ❑ Explain to the children that they will be learning what seeds need in order to grow into new plants.
- ❑ Tell them that the story they are going to listen to is a funny way of: 1) looking at the things plants need to grow, and 2) comparing them with some of the things we need to grow. Explain that the experiments the children are going to do after they've heard the story will be based on some of the questions the girl narrating the story asks her mother.
- ❑ Read the story (pages 15–17).
- ❑ Ask the children to help you list all the things the girl in the story found that plants need. Compare it with the list of things she found out that she needed (plus any others you discussed in work done on Unit 1A: Ourselves – see also the lesson plan on page 6).
- ❑ Show the children the resources you have collected and ask them to suggest experiments that could be done to test what plants need in order to grow. If they come up with some really good suggestions you could set them up straight away. Alternatively, they could carry them out once they have some more ideas, after doing the following experiment. In any case they need to do an experiment looking at the effect of light on growth at some stage.

Growing plants

We're going to set up an experiment to show what seeds need so they can grow into plants.

We need to know this because we need to grow plants for food.

We are learning how to record experimental results in a table.

We are going to carefully make observations or take measurements and record them in a table.

This is so other scientists can read our results.

❏ Ask them why it is important that we know how to grow plants. Explain to them that in the class experiment they are going to do, the class will be divided into eight groups, with two groups doing the same experiments each time. Ask them why it's good that more than one group is doing the same experiments. (Replicated experiments are more likely to avoid poor results when a particular experiment doesn't work/is set up wrongly – scientists will always repeat the same experiments several times over to check that it's correct)

❏ Explain that you want them to put some cotton wool into a container and then scatter a teaspoonful of seeds over it. Say that you want each group to use roughly the same amount of seeds and the same amount of cotton wool in each experiment. Ask them why they think you want this.

Group work

❏ Number the groups from 1 to 8. Choose which two groups will give their seeds no water, which will give a little water, which will give more water and which will fill the container with water. Ask each group to put a label on or near their container stating the group's number and 'No Water', 'Very little water', 'Some water' (half volume) or 'Full of water'.

❏ Ideally, when each group has set up their experiment, they should place all their containers in a similar place; for example, by the window. Ask the children why the containers should all be placed near each other. Stress the importance of keeping everything constant, the same, apart from the dependent variable (the factor being tested), the volume of water in this case.

❏ You will then need to give the seeds time to grow.

❏ When some of the seeds have begun to grow you could then give each child/pair/group a differentiated record sheet to record the results.

❏ Record sheet 1 asks the children to record growth or lack of growth with just a tick or a cross. Record sheet 2 requires the children to describe what happened (for example, 'The seeds grew a lot.') Record sheet 3 requires the children to measure the amount of growth.

Plenary

❏ Discuss the results of the experiments with the children. Remind them that the purpose of the lesson/experiment was to find out something about what seeds need to grow. What did they find out? How does what they've found out help us to know how to grow plants for food? How does what they've found out compare to what they found out in Unit 1 about how we need to look after ourselves?

Extension activities

❏ As intimated earlier, the children could grow the seeds in the light and away from the light and also in warm conditions and cold conditions. (Slightly surprisingly, some seeds need to be exposed to cold before they germinate; this is because they are exposed to cold conditions before the spring and use the cold as an environmental cue. Once they germinate all plants grow faster in warmer conditions!)

❏ The children could make a mind map showing the things plants need to be able to grow well.

'Why are you spraying water on the flowers?' I asked my mum one day. 'Is it to keep them clean, like I clean myself in the shower?'

'No, it's because they need water to live and it hasn't rained for quite a few days.'

I could see what my mum meant. The flowers in our neighbours' garden that hadn't been sprayed with water were all looking like the flowers Mum was given for her birthday a couple of weeks ago and had just taken out of her vases and thrown in the bin.

'Is that why I have to have a shower then, to help me live?'

'Well it is healthy to be clean but I'm watering the plants because the water goes down into the soil and the plants take in the water through their roots. You do need water to help you live as well though.'

'How do I get my water if I don't get it when I'm having a shower? I haven't got roots.'

'From the things you drink and the food you eat. Food often contains a lot of water.'

'Why do I have to eat?'

'The food helps you live as well as the water.'

Flowers

'Do the plants eat as well then? Shall I make them some toast?'

'They don't eat toast. They make the food they need from the air, water and the sun.'

'Do we get some of our food from the sun then? Is that why Auntie Alice sits in the sun all day? Are you full up when you go brown?'

'What a lot of questions! No, we can't make food from the sun like the plants do. Do you remember those potatoes we accidentally left in the cupboard for a long time? Do you remember how pale and sickly they looked?'

I did. Mum and I had planted them and quite soon the potatoes had bright green leaves, like normal plants. But to start with they looked like ghost plants.

'As to your Auntie Alice sunbathing, sunlight does affect us and we need it to be healthy – but we must remember to put sun cream on to protect our skin as well.'

'Is it healthy to talk a lot as well, like Auntie Alice does?'

'I think you'd still be healthy, even if you didn't talk as much as Alice,' replied my mum, smiling at me.

'What else do plants need to help them grow?' I asked.

'Well most plants grow better when it's warmer.'

'Does that mean I'd grow faster in a hot country?'

Mum laughed, then said, 'If there's enough water and light plants grow quicker in hot countries but you can grow just as fast when it's hot or it's cold. It's just usually more pleasant when it's warm. Now then, I've got to go indoors and do some work, so you can finish off watering the plants.'

So my mum left me to water the flowers. While I was watering them, I thought about how the flowers and I were very similar. We both needed things to keep us alive; we just got a lot of them in different ways from each other. I must be quite like a flower anyway because the man who runs the post office always calls me 'flower' whenever we go in there.

Name _____

Growing seeds

Use this record sheet to show whether the seeds grew or not in the experiments.

Did the seeds grow? Put a tick or a cross for each tray.

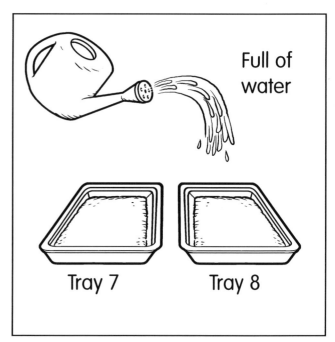

On the back of this sheet write what you found out by doing this test.

Name _____

Growing seeds

Use this record sheet to show whether the seeds grew or not in the experiments.

Did the seeds grow? Write down what happened in each tray.

No water:

Tray 1 _____

Tray 2 _____

A little water:

Tray 3 _____

Tray 4 _____

Some water:

Tray 5 _____

Tray 6 _____

Full of water:

Tray 7 _____

Tray 8 _____

On the back of this sheet write what you found out by doing this test.

Name _____

Growing seeds

Use this record sheet to show whether the seeds grew or not in the experiments.

Did the seeds grow? Measure in cm how much the seeds grew. Write the measurement down for each tray. (Note: you will probably have to write more than one measurement for each tray.)

No water:

Tray 1

Tray 2

Very little water:

Tray 3

Tray 4

Some water:

Tray 5

Tray 6

Full of water:

Tray 7

Tray 8

On the back of this sheet write what you found out by doing this test.

Science Scheme of Work objectives

Unit 1C: Sorting and using materials

Section 8: Choosing materials for a purpose

Section 9: Testing fabrics and papers

Section 10: Waterproof materials

To find out about the uses of a variety of materials and how these are chosen for specific purposes.

NC Sc3 1a, 1d

Background

This chapter looks at different materials and how well they fulfil a useful purpose, in this case being waterproof. As well as the children enjoying the story and the subsequent experiment, the lesson could be used to help them develop their skills of making predictions – a key scientific enquiry skill. To be a good scientist you have to wonder about things. 'I wonder if…?', 'I wonder what…?' and 'I wonder why…?' are the key questions that make the scientific world go round.

Einstein said, 'Imagination is everything,' which seems a fair comment from someone who could imagine what happens when you travel at light speed (such as time slowing down!) Children should understand that when we make predictions, we don't have to be correct. Our predictions just allow us to throw the stick forward and see what happens. A professional scientist is as excited to find out their prediction is wrong as to find out it is correct. More so even – they may have discovered that whatever it is they are studying is more interesting and complex than they thought. (Of course, it doesn't always work that way but the more we emphasise to the children that scientists should shout 'Hooray', whatever the results of their experiments, the less competitive or self-conscious they may be about making their predictions.)

The idea behind the story is that the three pigs are going camping and need to make clothes and tents. The first two pigs don't think carefully about the materials they use, or even

Resources

- Photocopiable record sheet (page 27)
- Squares of: toilet paper; newspaper; writing paper; cotton fabric, such as an old tea towel; plastic/nylon material, such as carrier bags
- Five equal sized plastic containers, such as cups
- Elastic bands
- Water trough or two fish tanks

What to do

We are learning about the properties of materials.

❏ Before the lesson set up the experiment that five of the children will demonstrate to the rest of the class. You need to put an equal volume of water in each of the five cups and then, using elastic bands, fasten each of the five materials to the top of each cup.

❏ Tell the children that you are going to tell them a story about the three little pigs (who in the original story had to choose suitable materials for a purpose – and failed in two cases!) Retell the original story if necessary. Say that this new story takes place a while after the pigs all ended up living in their stone house. The pigs are going on a camping holiday but as they don't have any camping clothes or a tent they have to make their own.

❏ Read the story (pages 23–26).

❏ Tell the children that you are going to do a similar test to the one that Thinky did. Show them the cups with the different sheets of material over the tops. Explain what the children who will be demonstrating the experiment are going to do. Ask the children why the cups you are using are all the same size and why you've put the same amount of water in each cup. (Fair test.)

❏ Then explain that first you want the children to make a prediction about which material will prove to be the most waterproof, by taking the longest to let the water out, and which will be the least waterproof. Explain that making predictions is a key part of being a scientist and that while we aim to make our predictions as accurately as possible, using the knowledge and experience that we have, it's all right if our predictions turn out not to be completely correct. Ask the children why this might be.

(It's because we have discovered – or are on the way to discovering – something new about the material we are testing that we didn't know about before. If we didn't make predictions and then test them we would never know if we were correct or find out that there are more interesting things for us to discover and learn.)

> What I'm looking for is for you to be able to predict and record the results of an experiment.

> This is because scientists often make predictions and then test them as a way of finding things out.

Individual, paired or group work

❑ Give out the record sheet to the children in groups, pairs or as individuals. Read it through with them. As a class discuss and then make a prediction about which will be the most waterproof material. Make sure the children write the name of that material as the first material on their list. Then let them predict the order of the other materials, from most waterproof to least waterproof. If they are working in pairs or groups, all the children should think about and discuss their predictions, rather than leaving the effort of predicting to the most outspoken members of the class. (Be sure to remind them that the best material will take the longest to leak!) There is only one record sheet in this unit, as the work will be differentiated by outcome.

❑ For the purpose of assessment and record keeping, the comments the children make to each other as they make their predictions could be recorded.

❑ Choose five children to each take one of the cups, ready to all invert them at the same time over the water tank at your signal. Ask the rest of the children to watch what happens very carefully. They need to see how quickly the water goes through each material (i.e. with the toilet paper probably straight away – the writing paper may last a surprisingly long time as it's usually waxed).

❑ Record the results on the board, showing which material proves to be the most waterproof and which the least. Ask the children to record the results on their sheets, compare them with their predictions and reflect on the accuracy of their predictions.

❑ Discuss with the children the success or otherwise of their predictions. Ask them which materials acted differently to how they'd predicted and ask them to consider why this might be so.

Plenary

❑ Review what the lesson involved – making predictions and then testing them. Remind the children that it didn't matter if their predictions were wrong but discuss why it was helpful to make predictions. In this case it would have caused the children to think about the properties of the materials and so think about why they might be more or less waterproof than others.

❑ Ask the children what the experiment showed about the materials and discuss what features of the materials made them waterproof or not waterproof.

❑ Review the story. Discuss how Speedy and Meedy lost out by not thinking carefully about what purpose they were using their materials for and how Thinky benefited from thinking about what purpose he was using the materials for and why he benefited from testing them before making his final choice – i.e. making a prediction and then testing it!

Extension activity

❑ Invite the children to suggest other materials to test and see how they compare to the most waterproof material. Materials could be: kitchen towels, glossy magazine paper, card, wrapping paper, large envelopes, used clothing and bubble wrap. Obviously, materials used for camping would have to have other properties; for example, being strong and warm. The children could be asked to design or suggest experiments to test these properties.

Now that they thought they were safe from the Wolf in their stone house, the Three Little Pigs decided to go on a camping holiday. As there aren't any camping shops in Fairyland, the three pigs decided to make their own camping clothes and their own tents.

Just like when they'd built their houses to protect themselves from the Big Bad Wolf, two of the pigs used materials that might not seem to you to be very sensible ones to use.

The first pig, who was called Speedy, didn't think about how camping clothes and tents might be used at all and made his clothes out of toilet paper and his tent out of newspaper. 'It's easy to cut and shape toilet paper into all sorts of interesting shapes and make fantastically fashionable clothes!' declared Speedy as he made himself all sorts of interesting looking outfits out of toilet paper. 'Newspaper is easy to fold and not very heavy to carry, so I think it's an ideal material to use for making a tent,' continued Speedy as he packed his newspaper tent into his

rucksack. Certainly his rucksack was very light to carry even with his large newspaper tent in it and several changes of very snazzy toilet paper clothes in it.

The Three Pigs Go Camping

The second pig, who was called Meedy, didn't think half enough about how camping clothes and tents might be used and he certainly didn't think about testing the materials he chose, to see if it was sensible to use them. So he made some camping clothes out of his tea towels and a tent using two of his duvets. 'I can't make toilet paper clothes that are quite as varied and interesting as those Speedy is making,' thought Meedy. 'But once I've stitched together a few of these tea towels, I bet my clothes will be much more suitable to wear for camping, as well as looking very smart on me. After all, it might get wet and windy and I bet my cotton clothes will be much warmer and more waterproof than his toilet paper clothes! I bet my two-duvet tent will make a much better tent than his newspaper tent – even if it does take up more space in my rucksack.'

Meanwhile, the third pig, who was called Thinky, was having a careful think about what materials to use to make his clothes and his tent from. He also had the sense to test the materials he'd thought of before using them to make sure he was right. He also tested the materials he saw his brothers using just in case they were better than the materials he'd chosen. As it happens the materials he thought of proved to be more waterproof in his test than the materials his brothers had chosen.

'Even though my clothes won't be as stylish as Speedy's toilet paper clothes, or even as smart as Meedy's tea towel clothes, I think I'll make my camping clothes out of plastic carrier bags tied together and I think I'll make my tent out of the plastic sheeting my new sofa was wrapped in, to protect it, when it was delivered to my stone house,' he decided after doing his tests.

When they got to the campsite, Speedy did indeed catch everyone's eye in his toilet paper clothes and his newspaper tent unfolded neatly and easily into shape, something else that impressed everyone.

Meanwhile, several campers commented on how smart Meedy looked in his tea towel outfits and how cosy his two-duvet tent looked.

In fact, Speedy and Meedy couldn't help feeling slightly ashamed and embarrassed by their brother who was wearing his odd looking carrier bag clothes and putting up his plain looking plastic sheet tent. They were glad when it was time to go to bed and they could pretend not to be with him.

That night though, it began raining. Only a little at first but it wasn't long before it was dripping through Speedy's newspaper tent and onto him. Wearing only his toilet paper clothes, he soon got very wet and very miserable.

When Speedy could stand it no more he begged Meedy to let him into his tent and to let him borrow some of his clothes. Meedy puffed out his chest with pride and

thought to himself how clever he'd been to make his clothes and his tent from more suitable materials.

It was at about this time that the rain got heavier. In a few minutes the tent made from two duvets was soaked and it collapsed on top of the two pigs inside it. The water from the tent seemed to soak straight through the tea towel clothes they were both shivering in.

It wasn't long before both of them begged Thinky to let them into his tent made of plastic sheeting and to let them borrow some of his carrier bag clothes.

As the rain lashed more heavily outside their tent, the pigs fell into a contented sleep because they were comfortably warm and dry.

They didn't know it but the Big Bad Wolf had been creeping up to their tent with the aim of catching them and eating them while they were asleep! But he'd now got so wet and miserable in his coat made of sponges glued together that he'd gone home to get warm and dry again.

It didn't stop him getting a nasty cold though – GOOD!

Name _____

Testing materials

You are going to test some of the materials that Thinky tested.

Before the experiment

Fill in the list below to show which material you predict will be the most
waterproof, through to the material you predict will be the least waterproof.

BEST   1. _____

               2. _____

               3. _____

               4. _____

WORST   5. _____

~~~~~~

After the experiment

Fill in the list to show which material proved to be the most waterproof in
the test, through to the material that was the least waterproof.

BEST   1. _____

               2. _____

               3. _____

               4. _____

WORST   5. _____

Was your prediction right? Circle the answer.   YES   NO

On the back of this sheet, describe or draw what happened
to the least waterproof material.

Light and dark

Science Scheme of Work objectives

Unit 1D: Light and dark

Covers all sections especially;

Section 7: Shiny objects and light sources

To identify different light sources, including the Sun. To sort objects into groups on the basis of simple material properties.

NC Sc4 3a, 3b

NC Sc3 1a, 1b, 1d

Background

This chapter examines light sources, reflective materials and non-reflective materials and their properties. In the narrative of the story the way that warm objects produce light is discussed, as is the fact that reflective materials are white or shiny. The surface of the Sun is 6000 °C (the core is even hotter!) and that heat produces the light that brightens up our day. Even small bulbs get very warm, so a point about safety is made in the story.

As you read and discuss the story you could ask the children what might cause a material to be non-reflective. (That it is dark and dull.)

Resources

- Photocopiable activity sheets 1–3 (pages 33–35)
- Examples of reflective materials, such as mirrors and shiny clothes

What to do

We are learning that certain things are light sources and that some materials reflect light and some don't.

❑ Tell the children that today's lesson will involve thinking about light sources; materials that reflect light (shiny) and those that are non-reflective (non-shiny). Tell them that after they have listened to the story and discussed it as a class, they will be making a list of light sources and materials that are reflective and non-reflective.

❑ Explain that the story is about a boy who wants to be a torch! Ask them to pay particular attention to the part in the story when Tom's mother Paula explains to him why he can't be a torch. He's not hot enough! (Actually, because we are warm creatures, we do emit a type of radiation – infra-red – which is similar to light! It is infra-red that 'night-time' goggles detect.) Tell them this will help them think about what things are light sources. Also ask them to listen carefully to what Paula tells Tom about reflective materials.

❑ Read the story (pages 30–32).

❑ Ask the children why Tom can't be a torch. Ask them to give you some examples of light sources. Can they remember how Paula describes shiny materials? Ask them to give you some examples of shiny materials. Can they tell you what the properties of non-reflective materials are? Ask them to give you some examples.

What I'm looking for is for you to recognise light sources, reflective materials and non-reflective materials.

This is because you need to know that different materials have different properties.

❑ Tell the children that they are going to use some worksheets to make a list of/distinguish between light sources, reflective materials and non-reflective materials.

Individual, paired or group work

❑ Give the children a copy of Activity sheet 1, 2 or 3, according to their ability to make a recording. Activity sheet 1 requires them to draw lines connecting drawings with the three definitions, light source, reflective and non-reflective. Activity sheet 2 is more challenging and requires the children to draw and categorise items into light sources, reflective materials and non-reflective materials. Activity sheet 3 is for children who can work independently to make three lists: light sources, reflective materials and non-reflective materials.

Plenary

❑ Review the purpose of the lesson. Ask the children to list some light sources. Ask them what makes them act as light sources. Ask them to list some reflective materials. Ask them what qualities these materials have that make them reflective. Ask them to list some non-reflective materials. Ask them what qualities these materials have that make them non-reflective. Discuss the results of the experiments with the children.

Extension activities

❑ Ask the children if they think the Moon is a light source. It does seem very bright! It isn't a light source because the Moon is very cold but it has a light coloured surface so it reflects the Sun's light. That's also why it seems to disappear when the Earth blocks the light from the Sun.

❑ Ask what the uses are for reflective and non-reflective materials because of these properties. For example, reflective clothes help people see us at night. The children could compare their effectiveness in a darkened room. (NB: reflective materials also reflect heat and are often used for this purpose; for example, silver cooking foil.)

❑ You could ask why many animals that are active at night time are a dark or black colour; for example, bats. Many fish have shiny scales so that as they swim, the light reflecting off the scales confuses predators.

Fifteen minutes after the ambulance had screeched past them in their car, Paula, Tom's mum, had finally convinced Tom that he couldn't be an ambulance, as he didn't have an engine inside him. Tom had a tendency to want to be things that had interested him and got his imagination going. It was shortly after this that they'd got the flat tyre.

There is never a good time to get a flat tyre but this time proved to be worse than usual. Paula was in a bit of a rush and, what was worse, they were in the middle of the countryside. It was night time and pitch black.

After Paula had shouted a bit, she called on her mobile phone to say she was going to be late. Then she calmed down a bit and asked for Tom's help to change the wheel.

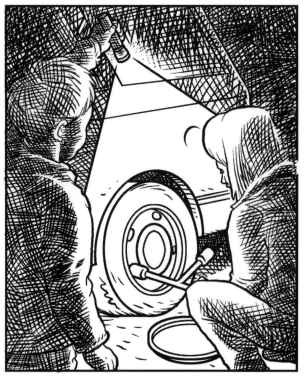

'I won't be able to see what I'm doing unless you shine the torch at the wheel with the flat tyre as I take it off and then at the spare tyre when I bolt it on,' she explained to Tom.

With the torch switched on, the tiny scene of his mum changing the wheel was brightly lit up and Tom watched fascinated as his mum changed the wheel. Tom had never seen a wheel on a car changed before and his mum clearly knew exactly how to do the job properly and safely.

'I had plenty of practice with the first cars I had when I was at college,' she told Tom.

By the time they were off on their journey again, Tom had decided he wanted to be a torch. 'I could see what you were doing so clearly and if we hadn't had the torch, we wouldn't have been able to change the wheel, would we?'

'That's certainly true,' his mum began. She was becoming an expert at explaining why Tom couldn't be certain things. 'But I think you'd find it difficult to be a torch.'

'Why's that?' asked Tom, sensing that another of his ideas wasn't going to work.

'Well, something gives out light when it's very hot, like a light bulb. That's why you should never touch a light bulb – even a small one – when it's on. The Sun gives out lots of light because it's very very hot. We say that they 'emit' light. You're not hot enough to emit light, I'm afraid.'

'What if I run all the way round the field and get very hot; couldn't I be a torch then?' asked Tom.

'Even then you wouldn't be hot enough to give out light, I'm afraid,' Paula replied.

Because she could tell that he was disappointed about this latest idea not working she tried to think of a way of encouraging him. 'You could be very good at helping torchlight if you wanted to, though,' she said.

'How could I do that?' asked Tom, brightening up.

'Well, if you wore white or shiny clothes, you could reflect light very well and that would spread the light around even further,' she explained.

'What does 'reflect' mean?' asked Tom.

'It means the light bounces off something, a bit like a ball bounces off a wall. When we get home how about we try and see which of your clothes reflect light the best?'

So when they got home later that night that's exactly what they did. Paula switched off the lights in the sitting room, and then shone a torch at Tom who tried on different clothes in order to be a torchlight-reflector. Paula's prediction that white or shiny clothes would reflect the light best proved to be correct. (Tom tried wearing a black T-shirt and that hardly reflected the torchlight at all!) Tom decided he liked being a torchlight-reflector in his white and shiny clothes. He also realised he'd be safer in the dark wearing his shiny clothes. Paula was glad that Tom had finally found something to be that he **could** be!

Name _____

Light and dark

Below are some pictures of light sources, reflective materials and non-reflective materials.

Draw a line from each picture to the words that best describe it.

Light source

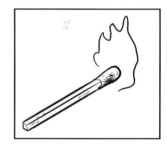

Reflective (shiny) material

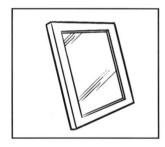

Non-reflective (non-shiny) material

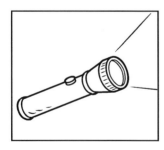

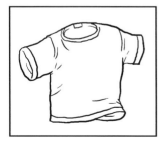

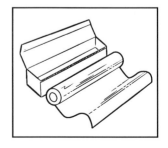

Name _____

Light and dark

In the boxes below draw some light sources, reflective (shiny) materials and non-reflective (non-shiny) materials. Write underneath which each one is. Make sure you draw some of each.

Two pictures have been done to start you off.

Name _____

Light and dark

Make a list of all the light sources, reflective materials and non-reflective materials you can think of.

Light sources	Reflective/shiny materials	Non-reflective/non-shiny materials

Pushes and pulls

Science Scheme of Work objectives

Unit 1E: Pushes and pulls

Covers all sections, particularly;

Section 3: Pushing and pulling objects

To know that both pushes and pulls are examples of forces.

NC Sc4 2b

Background

This chapter looks at pushes and pulls and how these two forces can be made more effective. In the activities that follow the story the children are asked to think about twists, which are a combination of a pull and a push. (If you were twisting a round door handle to the right or left, you'd be pushing the top of it and pulling the underneath of it.) In the story, where Hare and Tortoise compete to push a stone from one side of the forest to the other, Hare just relies on brute strength whereas Tortoise finds ways of making his stone easier to push or pull (and inevitably wins!) Tortoise makes things easier for himself by clearing obstacles out of his path, moving his stone down onto a smoother surface and wrapping a vine around it so he can pull instead of push (pulling is usually more efficient than pushing – that's why horses go at the front of carts!). After a brief uphill struggle he manages to

Resources

• Photocopiable activity sheets 1–3 (pages 41–43)

What to do

We are learning that pushes, pulls and twists are forces.

❏ Explain to the children that the lesson will be about learning about the forces called pull, push and twist. Tell them that the story is about another

competition between Hare and Tortoise. Make sure they know the original story and then explain that in this new race the two animals have to push a stone from one side of the forest to the other. Tell them that all Hare does in the story is use his strength to push his stone but Tortoise thinks of several ways to make it easier to move his stone. Ask the children to listen carefully and see if they can spot the methods Tortoise uses.

❏ Read the story (pages 38–40).

❏ Ask the children to recount the ways in which Tortoise made it easier for himself to move his stone. Ask them why those methods worked. Some children will be able to understand that, while you can have an equal pulling force or pushing force, it is usually easier to pull something with more force than push something with the same force. (You could mention horses at the front of carts/train engine usually being at the front of a row of carriages.)

❏ Ask the children to imagine turning a round door knob (get them to do it if you have one!) Ask them if the twisting action is a push or a pull. Explain to them that it involves both forces.

❏ Tell the children that the activities they are going to do involve two tasks. First they have to make drawings of Hare moving his stone and/or some of the ways Tortoise made his stone easier to move. Then they have to decide whether the use of the forces illustrated or described on the worksheets involves pushes, pulls or twists.

What I'm looking for is for you to know the difference between pushes, pulls and twists.

This is because you need to understand the language of forces and how they can be used to make life easier.

Individual, paired or group work

❏ Activity sheet 1 asks the children to draw how Hare moved his stone and one way Tortoise made it easier to move his stone. The second activity is a series of illustrations of forces being used and asks the children to circle the correct force from a choice of three. Activity sheet 2 asks the children to draw how Hare moved his stone and two ways Tortoise made it easier to move his stone. The second activity is a series of illustrations of forces being used and asks the children to write under each one the name of the force being used. Activity sheet 3 asks the children to draw three ways Tortoise made it easier to move his stone. The second activity is a chart of movements. The children are asked to complete the chart to show what force is being used each time.

Plenary

❏ Review the story. How did Hare move his stone? What problems did he have? How did Tortoise make it easier to move his stone? Why did his methods work? What types of force does a twist involve? What makes something harder to push? What makes something easier? What difference does a slope make?

❏ You could also ask whether the race was fair. In one respect it was but Tortoise used his knowledge of science to turn the odds to his favour!

Extension activity

❏ An interesting thing to discuss is which forces are involved in opening a door. It can depend on all sorts of things as doors can open inwards or outwards! Maybe the children could examine and record the differences between the doors around the school.

All the animals in the wood teased Hare so much about losing his race with Tortoise that he organised another race against him. This time, though, he made it more difficult because the two animals had to move a heavy stone from one side of the wood to the other.

As soon as Badger shouted 'Go!' Hare began pushing his stone as hard as he could. He was amazed to notice that Tortoise hadn't started pushing his stone but had walked around to the other side of it.

'Why… is… he… doing that…?' Hare thought to himself, wondering why his stone seemed to be getting harder and harder to push.

What Tortoise was doing was clearing the path for his stone. Hare was having to work very hard because three pebbles were caught up on the other side of his stone, making it much harder to push. In fact it wasn't until Tortoise caught up with him, looking much less tired, that Hare realised what Tortoise was doing by stopping every now and again to clear his path.

Hare was beginning to think it was going to be harder to beat Tortoise than he had thought, when to his delight he saw Tortoise pushing his stone sideways. He was pushing it off the pebbly path and into the smooth and dried-up path that ran alongside the pebbly path for a while.

Hare couldn't imagine why Tortoise was wasting his time pushing the stone in the wrong direction. 'Lucky for me he seems to be madder than a March hare… hee hee,' thought Hare.

Of course, Tortoise knew what he was doing. He knew the stone would be easier to push along the smooth surface of the dried-up path.

Tortoise soon started catching up with Hare, who by this time had *had* to stop and rest. He couldn't believe his eyes when he noticed Tortoise making steady progress towards him! He was going to panic but then he noticed that Tortoise had stopped again. To his amazement he noticed Tortoise start chewing through a low growing vine.

'Why's he stopped for lunch?' thought Hare. 'At least I've only stopped for a quick rest!' Then off Hare went again, puffing and panting as he pushed his stone.

Tortoise hadn't stopped for lunch. He'd realised that if he wrapped the vine around his stone he could pull his stone instead of pushing it. As he began pulling his stone he soon started catching up with Hare.

The now exhausted Hare looked behind him to see Tortoise steadily gaining on him as he pulled his stone along. The two animals had come to a fork in the path through the woods. Hare couldn't believe his luck when he noticed that Tortoise was turning up the route that led uphill to Badger's Rise.

'What a fool Tortoise is!' thought Hare. 'Anyone can tell it's easier to move something along a level surface than to move it up a slope.'

For once Hare was right. By the time tired Tortoise finally got to the top of Badger's Rise, Owl, who was watching the race from above the trees, was able to see that Hare was well ahead. But from Badger's Rise it was downhill all the way! So Tortoise began pushing his stone downhill and as soon as he did, he could hardly keep up with it!

The finish line was just a little way beyond where the two paths came out of the trees. When a very tired Hare came out of the woods along his path, there was no sign of Tortoise. Even though he wanted to finish the race, Hare was so exhausted he just had to curl up and have a quick nap. 'Surely this time it won't matter if I have a rest,' he thought.

Just as Hare was beginning to dream about fields full of dandelions, Tortoise came into view from between the trees. To the cheers of all the animals waiting at the finish line, Tortoise steadily pushed his stone along until the race was won!

Name _____

Pushes, pulls and twists

Draw one picture to show how Hare moved his stone and one picture to show one of the ways Tortoise moved his stone.

Circle 'push', 'pull' or 'twist' for each of the pictures below.

push   pull   twist

push   pull   twist

push   pull   twist

push   pull   twist

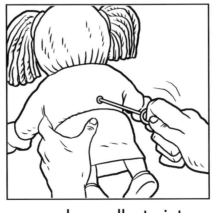
push   pull   twist

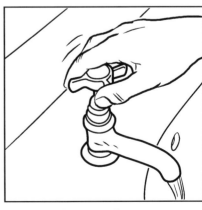
push   pull   twist

Name _____

Pushes, pulls and twists

Draw one picture to show how Hare moved his stone and two pictures to show some of the ways Tortoise made his stone easier to move.

The drawings below show some forces being used.
Write under each one the name of the force that is being used.

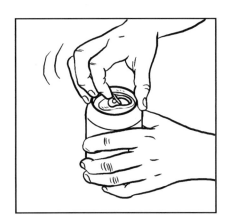

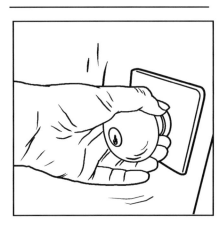

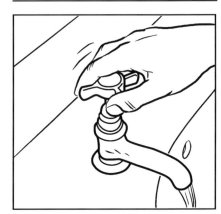

Name _____

Pushes, pulls and twists

Draw some pictures to show the different ways Tortoise made his
stone easier to move. Write a caption for each picture.

_____   _____   _____

_____   _____   _____

Complete the chart below to show what force is being used each time. One has been
done for you.

Type of movement	Force being used
moving a shopping trolley	push
a reindeer moving a sleigh	
opening a drink can	
opening a fridge door	
working a tap	
opening a screw top on a bottle	
opening a crisp packet	
moving a child in a buggy	
a horse moving a cart	
using a screwdriver	

Sound and hearing

Science Scheme of Work objectives

Unit 1F: Sound and hearing

Covers all sections especially:

Section 3: Making different sounds

Section 6: How we hear

Section 9: Testing sound and distance

To know that there are many kinds of sound and sources of sound. To know that sounds travel away from sources, getting fainter as they do and that they are heard when they enter the ear.

NC Sc2 2g

NC Sc4 3c, 3d

Background

In this lesson the children explore how sound is made by something vibrating, that it's our ears that allow us to hear and that as we move away from a sound source, the sound becomes quieter.

Sound has to travel through a medium – which is why the film advertisement that claimed, 'In space no one can hear you scream,' was actually a good one. Normally we hear things because of sound travelling through the air but actually the denser the medium, the better sound travels. That's why in all the old B-Westerns the Injuns* were always listening to the ground to hear if any riders were nearby, because the ground carries the sound. That's why a tuning fork sounds louder when you put it on a table – the sound travels through the table making it vibrate as well as the air. It's also why Beethoven was able to carry on composing when he was nearly deaf because he leant his ear against his piano.

For the following activities the class could be divided into three mixed-ability investigative groups using a carousel system that means they all engage in the three investigations. For this purpose there are three record sheets, one for each investigation, that are not differentiated by ability.

*Native Americans

Resources

- Record sheets for each investigation (pages 49–51)
- Tuning forks (about five)
- Glasses/cups with water in them
- Music system
- Different sized 'elephant ears' (false ears of different sizes made, for example, from card – about five pairs)
- Different sized balloons (or balloons blown up to different sizes! – about five)
- A drum, tambourine or similar instrument

What to do

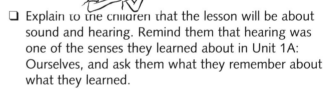

We are learning that sound is caused when something vibrates and how sounds travel.

❑ Explain to the children that the lesson will be about sound and hearing. Remind them that hearing was one of the senses they learned about in Unit 1A: Ourselves, and ask them what they remember about what they learned.

❑ Tell them that in the story they are about to hear about Mrs Millet, she uses her knowledge of sound and hearing to make her life even happier than it is already. Ask them to listen to the story very carefully and see if they can explain to you what it is about sound and hearing that Mrs Millet knows about.

❑ Read the story (pages 46–48).

❑ Ask the children if they spotted the things Mrs Millet knew about sound and hearing that meant she could no longer hear her husband moaning while he ate his dinner.

Individual, paired or group work

❑ Tell the children that they will be carrying out three investigations and that you will be providing them with record sheets for each investigation. You could introduce each investigation through whole class demonstrations, especially if you have no classroom assistants. Alternatively, with the use of assistants, each investigation could be demonstrated to the children as they get to it. Before letting them start, ask the children what 'vibrating' means. Look it up in a dictionary. Write the word and the definition on the board.

What I'm looking for is for you to be able to explain how sounds are made and how well they travel.

This is because we need to understand the world around us.

Investigation 1

- The children are to investigate the sound created by a tuning fork. Ask them to:

  1. Tap the tuning fork against a table and then hold it close to their ear.

  2. Tap the tuning fork against a table and then place the base on the table. (After a while they could place their ear against the table.)

  3. Tap the tuning fork against a table and then hold it gently on their nose or against their arm.

  4. Tap the tuning fork against a table and then place the tip of it in a glass of water.

     (NB: children love this but obviously it makes a bit of a mess so you may need a plastic cover on the table!)

- Ask the children what they noticed in each activity and why putting the tuning fork in the water made the water splash about everywhere!

- Ask them to complete Record sheet 1.

Investigation 2

- Ask the children to sit facing the music system as you play a piece of music or the radio. Tell them this investigation is about finding out about how we hear things. Discuss the fact that the volume of the music will naturally go up and down but that using the different sized 'elephant ears' you want them to decide which 'elephant ears' help them hear the best after carefully listening to the music for a while.

- Ask them to also listen with their hands cupped around their ears and see if that helps them hear any better than normal (or even better than when they're using the 'elephant ears' – if it does, ask them why this might be. Maybe they can make their hands mould around their ears better than the cardboard ears!)

- Ask the children to tell you what they noticed. Then, ask them to work in pairs to whisper to each other while using the 'elephant ears' to find out when they can hear the whispering most easily.

- Ask the children to tell you what they found out and then ask them to complete their Record sheet 2. As they are record sheets rather than worksheets, they are not differentiated; however, the work they do will be differentiated by outcome. The work will be a great opportunity to assess and record what the children say, i.e. the real science that is taking place.

Investigation 3

- Ask the children to work in pairs. Using one balloon at a time, ask one of each pair to hold the balloon to their ear. (**Safety:** make sure the balloons are not blown up so much that they might burst and cause damage to the hearing. The children must be warned not to squeeze them.) Ask their partner to whisper against the other side of the balloon. Which balloon did the sound travel through the best? Ask the children to write about this on Record sheet 3.

- Then take the children into the playground or the hall. Stand at one end of the area with the children standing close to you. Play beats of equal volume on the drum. Ask the children to slowly move away from you and stop when they can't hear you playing the drum any more. (Some children may claim they can still hear you when they're the other side of the hall. Ask them what they noticed about what happened to how loud the sound became as they moved away from you!) They should write what happened on Record sheet 3.

Plenary

❑ Ask the children what they noticed in each investigation and why they think they noticed the results that they did.

❑ Ask them to help you make a list of all the things that made sounds during your lesson today (the tuning forks, music centre, them (!), the drum).

Mrs Millet

Mrs Millet loved her husband. He worked hard all day, often bought her thoughtful little presents and helped with the household chores. Like some people, though, he liked to have a bit of a moan now and again.

Mr Millet did his moaning at the dinner table. If there was anything he wanted to get off his chest he moaned between munches. It was the only time of day when Mrs Millet didn't enjoy being in Mr Millet's company. She would much rather have talked about poetry, the beautiful sunrise that morning, sport or most especially about her favourite subject, which was science. But no, Mr Millet would just moan, moan, moan. Like most people who like a good moan, Mr Millet didn't really have much to moan about, so his complaints were usually quite silly.

A typical mealtime might start with Mrs Millet asking, 'Are you enjoying your meal, dear?'

To which Mr Millet would usually reply by saying something like, 'Do you realise cows and bulls don't have to go to school?'

'No dear,' Mrs Millet might reply.

'Or sheep… or goats… not even chickens. We should really do more to educate the nation's livestock… Why, if I was in charge…'

Mr Millet would continue like this, explaining for the rest of their meal how he would solve things like the shortage of rainbows, the problem of litter that couldn't throw itself away and how to get cows into the classroom.

When Mrs Millet realised that she could stand no more of her husband's moaning, she decided to use what she knew about the science of sound to help make her dinner times more peaceful.

Because she knew that the sounds we hear mainly travel through the air and into our ears, she would put a little bit of cotton wool in her ears before each meal. Even though that helped block out most of the sound of Mr Millet's moaning, it didn't cut it out completely, so she had to use some more science to help her.

Every day for a week, bit by bit so her husband wouldn't notice, Mrs Millet made the kitchen table a little bit longer. That meant that by the end of the week the table was quite a lot longer. Mrs Millet knew that as sound spreads out through the air, it gets quieter and quieter the further you are away from where the sound is coming from.

So from then on Mr Millet could moan to his heart's content about ducks not swimming upside down or cats never sweeping the road, while Mrs Millet, who couldn't hear him any more, could enjoy her meal and think about how much she appreciated her husband for volunteering to do the ironing after dinner.

That meant that thanks to Mrs Millet's knowledge of science the Millets lived happily ever after.

Name _____

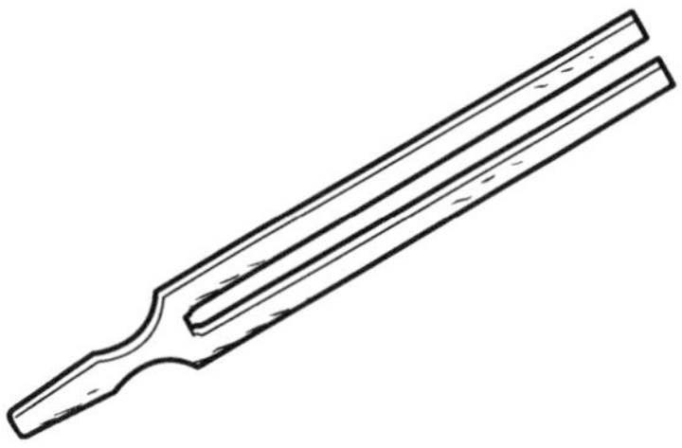

Investigation 1

Testing a tuning fork

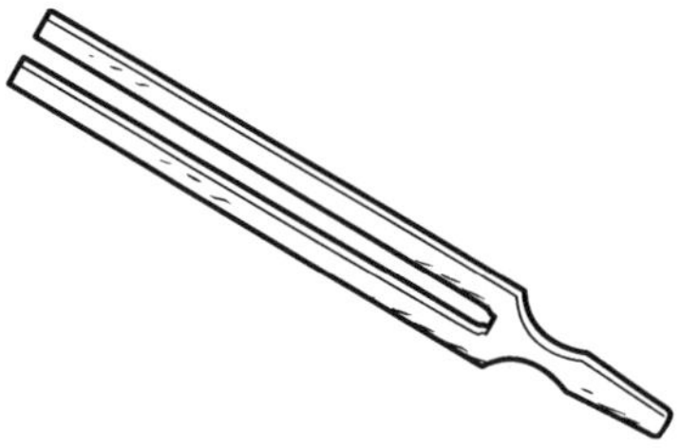

Draw what happened when you put the tuning fork in the water.

Complete this sentence.

Water splashed **everywhere** because the tuning fork was

_____.

Name _____

Investigation 2

Elephant ears

Which ears heard the music best? _____

Why? _____

Which ears heard the whispering best? _____

Why? _____

Name _____

Investigation 3

Balloons and drums

With which balloon was the sound

loudest? _____

Why? _____

_____

_____

_____

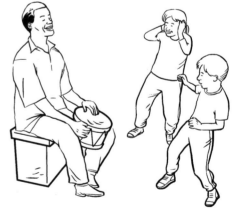

What happened as you moved away from the drum?

_____

Why? _____

_____

_____

_____

Problems for Princess Puzzle

'Where is that soon-to-be-my-husband of mine?' demanded Princess Puzzle as she stormed around the gardens of the palace trying to find Prince Book. She was followed, as usual, by her two wizards, Wizard Why? and Wizard What?. Princess Puzzle usually just called them 'Why?' and 'What?'.

'I bet he's got his head buried in yet another book,' thought Princess Puzzle out loud as she looked behind a rose bush. All Prince Book thought about was reading… that and football. He read a lot of books and comics about football.

'Why are you looking for him?' asked Why?.

'What if he's not here and he's having a doze in his bedchamber?' asked What?.

Princess Puzzle was just about to hurl answers back at the two wizards (she was used to them asking questions all the time) when a very worried page ran up to her.

'Milady, Mi – puff, pant, cough, wheeze – lady,' began the breathless page as he knelt on one knee before her. 'I bring bad news…'

'Don't tell me Cook's burnt the scones again!' interrupted Princess Puzzle.

'Far worse than that, Milady. Tha…' continued the page, trying to explain.

'Oh no! Don't tell me the housemaid's washed my green knickers with my red knickers so I've got yellow knickers again!' shrieked Princess Puzzle, interrupting again.

'No! It's worse than that! You see…'

'My goodness! *Surely* you're not going to tell me the cat's jumped up on my throne chasing a mouse, so it needs polishing again like it did last time?' asked the princess, interrupting a third time.

'**NO!!!**' shouted the page, trying to get the Princess to shut up and to give her his message. 'It's far far worse than that! You remember that awful ugly ogre who wanted to marry you, called Yuck?'

'Oh **Yuck**. Yes, I remember him… Ah! He was absolutely **Yuck** that Yuck,' replied the princess.

'Well, after he learned that you were planning to marry Prince Book, he grabbed him and ran off with him to his castle. He's bolted the huge gates to his horrible castle and says he won't let Prince Book out unless you marry him instead!'

'Me? Marry Yuck? **YUCK!** That would be horrible! **Yuck!** Even though he's always reading, just like all the men around here, I love my little Prince Book. We'll have to save him!'

'How?' asked Why?.

'I don't know,' replied Princess Puzzle.

'What if we go and look at the ogre's castle?' asked What?. 'That might give us some ideas.'

'Great idea! Right, page, tell the cook to pack us some scones and the housekeeper to pack some of my green knickers… oh and don't forget to feed that pesky cat while we're gone,' said the princess.

'Yes Milady,' said the page, glad he'd finally been able to pass on his message and get his breath back.

~~~~~~

A little while later, Princess Puzzle and the two wizards were standing outside the ugly ogre's castle. It wasn't a very pleasant place to stand for two reasons. For one reason, they could tell from where they were standing that the door to the ogre's castle was very very strong. It would be very difficult to break it down and rescue the prince. The other reason was that there was rubbish of all kinds scattered about all over the place outside the castle. It was like an untidy scrapyard where a spoilt baby giant had thrown around its toys. There were bits of aluminium girder from some kind of machine or other. There were thick poles of wood that looked like they might have once been telegraph poles. There were long thick tubes of plastic and concrete that looked like they were supposed to be water pipes.

'Right. Well, we'll need to use something to batter the door down, like a battering ram. We'll use those metal girders because they'll be the strongest!' the princess commanded.

'What if they're not the strongest?' asked What?.

'Why don't we test all the poles, girders and tubes?' asked Why?.

'Oh *all right*,' replied Princess Puzzle, impatiently. She just wanted to get on with rescuing the prince. 'But I know metal's very strong, so I'm sure it'll be the strongest!'

'Maybe you're right,' agreed Why?.

'But what if we find something else is stronger?' added What?.

'*OK… OK…* Let's get on with this testing, shall we?' asked the princess, testily.

There were lots of planks of wood lying about all over the place. Princess Puzzle picked up one of the metal girders and smashed it against one of the thinnest planks. The plank smashed to pieces. Then she picked up one of the plastic tubes and smashed it against one of the thickest planks of wood. That made a loud noise but it didn't smash the plank of wood.

'There we are… I told you the metal girders would be best. Can we get on now?' asked the princess, even more impatiently. She *desperately* wanted to get on with battering the door down.

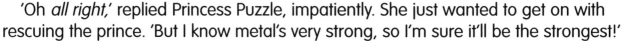

'But that wasn't a fair test,' said Why?. 'The planks of wood you were hitting weren't the same.'

'Why, you didn't even test all of the things we could use,' added What?.

'**Oh...** *all right...* We'll test all the materials on similar planks of wood!' agreed the princess knowing she needed the two wizards to help her and that they'd never get anywhere until they'd done the experiments the wizards wanted to do. To her surprise they found that when they tested all the materials the wooden poles proved the strongest the most often.

'Metal *is* very strong,' said Why?, supportively.

'Out of the materials we've got, the wooden poles are just the strongest for doing *this* job,' added What?.

Well, the princess and her two trusty (and wise) wizards used the wooden poles that had proved the strongest in their tests and after a little while they'd broken down the door to the ogre's castle. This was lucky because they discovered that the ogre had popped out to the supermarket but was expected back at any moment.

'If we hadn't done those fair tests to find out the best material to use, we could still have been trying to batter the door down with materials that weren't strong enough, until we used the wooden pole,' said Princess Puzzle as she, the prince and the wizards dashed back to the safety of her palace.

'Why don't we always do tests like that?' asked Why?.

'What a good idea!' said What?.

So they always did fair tests like that ever after.

Notes on the story

Problems for Princess Puzzle

When discussing this story, you could look at the way in which the tests were unfair because of the situation the characters were in and also how they conducted their tests.

As a result of the situation they were in, the characters had a random mix of materials. To do a fair test, they would have used materials of the same shape and size.

The princess did the tests unfairly because:

- she tested the strength of the metal girder and the plastic tube on different thicknesses of wood;
- she didn't test all the available materials.

Being aware of these pitfalls, you and your children could design a fair test to compare the qualities of some materials (see the Materials chapter on page 21).